CURRENT AFFAIRS

The Nazis in Scandinavia

ISSUED FORTNIGHTLY BY THE

ARMY BUREAU OF CURRENT AFFAIRS

RESTRICTED

The information given in this publication is not to be communicated, either directly or indirectly, to the Press or to any person not authorised to receive it.

No. 69   May 20th, 1944

THE NAZIS IN SCANDINAVIA

K. Kenney, T. M. Terkelsen & R. Bennett

BooksUlster

First published by the Army Bureau of Current Affairs 1944–45. This compilation published by Books Ulster in 2016.

Typographical arrangement © Books Ulster

ISBN: 978-1-910375-52-5

Editor's Note

This publication comprises two articles, 'The Nazis in Scandinavia' and 'Northern Neighbour' (Norway), originally published by the (British) Army Bureau of Current Affairs in 1944 and 1945 respectively. ABCA was 'created by the Army Council to "brief" officers for talks to their men on war topics and to provide them with informative "background" on varied aspects of the war.' Its *Current Affairs* and *War* series provided the basis for debate within groups of service personnel.

SCANDINAVIAN CONTRASTS

I. MAILED FIST OR VELVET GLOVE?

THIS bulletin offers a study of the Nazi technique of enslavement well worth examining with your group. The Nazis first tried out in Norway their now familiar set-up of a Quisling, supported by a local Nazi party and the Gestapo, using ruthless brutality against all forms of resistance. Conquered Denmark, on the other hand, was designed as a "Model Protectorate," allowed to run on its own lines but expected to collaborate with a benevolent Germany in Europe's New Order.

What success did Hitler have with either technique?

II. WHY THE DIFFERENCE?

The contrast—until recently—between the German treatment of Norway and Denmark has puzzled many. Was it because the Norwegians made a more determined stand against the invasion of April 9th, 1940? Why was the fighting over in a few hours in Denmark, while Norwegian forces held out for over two months? Surely geography had a great deal to do with it? (pp. 4–6, 14).

Again, why did King Christian stay with his cabinet in Denmark, and not escape abroad like his brother, King Haakon and the Government of Norway? (pp. 14–15). Are the Danes allies, or neutrals, or what? (p. 19).

Did treachery play any real part in the fall of each country? Or was the dirty work almost entirely on the German side? (pp. 4–6).

III. WHY GO TO NORWAY AT ALL?

Can we, with the aid of a map of Europe, work out the motives for the German invasion of Norway? Mr. Kenney suggests three reasons:

(i) to exploit the country's strategic possibilities and forestall the remote chance of a flank attack by the Allies;

(ii) to secure the county's economic resources;

(iii) to nazify the population by means of Quisling and his "Hirdmen."

These points can be illustrated from the facts given here in (e.g.: (i) the fjords for U-boat bases and for hiding battleships: what happened to the *Tirpitz*, by the way? (ii) the fishing-fleets, merchant ships and oil-tankers: but did the Germans get hold of many of these?) (pp. 5, 11)

IV. HAS THE NORWAY EXPERIMENT PAID?

Offsetting the obvious advantages to Germany of raw materials, supplies and compulsory labour for her war-machine, ask your group whether the worry and expense of keeping large forces tied down on Scandinavian soil, plus the Gestapo, spies, informers and the rest, have been worth while?

Resistance started at once: who were the leaders? The lawyers, the clergy, the teachers, the trade unionists, the journalists.

And the results of German occupation?

1. Quisling has become the most contemptible word in the Norwegian language.

2. The Norwegians are determined that "never again" shall Germany be in a position to threaten their country.

Was it worth it, Adolf?

V. AND WHAT ABOUT DENMARK?

What things do members of your group associate with Denmark? Bacon and eggs? Danish butter? Co-operative farms? Anybody heard of the Folk High Schools and the way they have practised ABCA for a hundred years? (pp. 11–14).

All these added up to make a well-run, prosperous and freedom-loving little democracy—until the Nazis came.

VI. IS IT A MODEL PROTECTORATE?

What do the Germans get out of Denmark—food, war-workers, money? (pp. 14–15). Observe that the Nazis pay for nothing—it's all down in the books at the bank: debts that will never be honoured.

Has Danish democracy survived? After a fashion for a while—in a Parliamentary election permitted by the Nazis less than 2 per cent. of the voters supported the Danish Nazi Party. And underground the Council of Freedom is equally upholding the spirit of Danish democracy (p. 15–16). Sabotage, as Mr. Terkelsen says, has become a fine art. And the resistance movement is getting ready for the armies of liberation.

VII. ABJECT FAILURE OF A MASTER RACE

In Norway the Nazis have failed to get any popular support for their tool, Quisling. And they can never relax for a moment.

In Denmark, the mixture of threats and cajolery which supported the Model Protectorate has given place to the more usual blood and iron tactics. What's been going on there since August, 1943: is the King still free? And the Government? What happened to the Army? And how did the Danish Navy avoid falling into German hands? (pp. 16–19).

The fight is on, in Denmark, too. She is an ally in all but name and, like Norway, she is waiting.

The Nazis in Scandinavia

By K. Kenney (Norway) and T. M. Terkelsen (Denmark).

(From ABCA Current Affairs, No. 69, May 20th, 1944)

I. The People of Norway

1. They Live Among Mountains and Fjords

IF you wish to understand a people, examine the country they live in. This is even more true of Norway than of most countries, for the individual nature of this craggy land of mountains, fells, tumbling rivers and calm pine-fringed lakes is so strong that the human being who has grown up there carries certain characteristics implanted within him to his dying day.

Norway is a long narrow land running roughly NNE—SSE. From its southernmost point to its northern tip is 1,100 miles—as far as from London to Naples—while its coastline is so indented by fjords and islands that the total length of coastline is 12,000 miles. The high mountains and fells on the west coast make overland communications a real problem. Until quite recently, the yeomen farmers in Norway's mountain valleys were almost completely cut off from towns and cities during the winter and lived a simple and almost self-supporting life in their snowbound farms; in consequence they became accustomed to rely on themselves and develop a sturdy independence of outlook.

2. The Sea Is In Their Blood

The North Sea and the Atlantic, which wash the coasts of Southern and Northern Norway respectively, have also had a deep effect on the Norwegian character. A thousand years ago they offered the Norwegian Vikings contact with the outside world—they were, so to say, front doors to the Shetlands and Orkneys, to Iceland, Greenland and Vinland (Massachusetts) in the North, and southwards to England, France, the Canaries and the Mediterranean as far east as Constantinople. In more recent times the sheltered waters inside the west coast skerries have offered easier means of communication than the land, so that (particularly in the south), rowing boats and motor launches are to the Norwegians what the push-bike is to the British working man, while the relatively thickly populated coast is serviced by a network of coastal steamer routes.

The rich fisheries off the Norwegian coast and Norwegian enterprise in the field of whaling made the Norwegian fishing industry the most important in Europe (the average catch used to be over 1,000,000 tons yearly), and provided a valuable export for Norway's overseas trade. The sea has soaked deeply into Norwegian blood, and that accounts for Norway's remarkable pre-war position in ocean commerce. This tiny nation of 3,000,000 people owned and operated the fourth largest merchant shipping fleet in the world (nearly 5,000,000 tons deadweight), with the highest proportion of modern vessels and tankers of any merchant navy.

3. They Treasured Their Independence

A superficial glance at Norway's history is enough to show the basis of a third dominating trait in the Norwegian national character—intense love of personal and national freedom. From the end of the fourteenth century until 1814 Norway was united to Denmark under conditions amounting to virtual subjugation, and the history of that period is filled with the struggles of the Norwegian population to assert its national character and culture in the face of the Danish ruling caste and bureaucracy. In 1814, after the Napoleonic Wars, the King of Denmark was forced to renounce his sovereignty over Norway in favour of the Swedish King; and the Norwegians seized the opportunity to call a national assembly at Eidsvold and to draw up a national constitution, based on the French revolutionary concept of "Liberty, Equality and Fraternity" and modelled closely on the American Constitution.

Although Norway continued to be bound unwillingly to Sweden and the Norwegian State had to struggle vigorously for its rights, the Constitution remained in force; the Norwegians had asserted their right to settle their own destiny, and had laid the foundations for the free democratic state which was to emerge at the beginning of the twentieth century. In 1905 a dispute over Norway's rights to establish a separate Norwegian consular service decided the Norwegian Government to proclaim the dissolution of the Union with Sweden, and by a plebiscite Prince Carl of Denmark was elected King of Norway. The Swedish Government sensibly accepted the situation, and on November 18th, 1905, Prince Carl formally became King of Norway under the name of Haakon VII.

4. They Built a Modern Democracy

Norway, then, had won her place in the Scandinavian group of States. The main features of these States were their strongly democratic outlook and constitutions, the high place accorded by them to internal social development, the traditional classlessness of their society, and the smooth, orderly reasonableness of their mode of life. Symptomatic of Norway's "social-democratic" outlook was the attention devoted to her social services (which consumed one-third of her municipal revenues), the strength and solidarity of her organised labour (12 per cent. of her entire population were members of the trade union movement), her concentration on education (all State education in Norway, from elementary school to University, was free, and there were almost no private schools), and the nation's interest in the press (the production of newspapers and periodicals *per capita*, was the highest in the world).

II. What Happened in 1940, and Why

1. Neutrality Had Become a Tradition

Norway, like the other Scandinavian States, managed to remain neutral during the first world war, and her merchant navy earned good money for the owners and the Norwegian State on charter to the Allies. During the post-war years Norway was a convinced and firm supporter of the League of Nations, but when the policy of collective security broke down, Norway, with the other states signatory to the Oslo Convention, withdrew into disillusioned isolationism and neutrality. During the years before the present war the doctrine of neutrality became almost an obsession with Norwegians, and this, combined with the feeling that "it can't happen here," gave a very unreal flavour to the Norwegian conception of the country's position at the outbreak of war in 1939.

For the first seven months of war Norway tottered precariously on the edge of the precipice. The major threat to good relations with the Allies was presented by the transport of Swedish iron ore from the Norwegian port of Narvik and southwards inside Norwegian territorial waters. Sweden supplied Germany with some 9,000,000 tons annually of high-grade ore; of this about one-fourth passed through Narvik, a traffic which was viewed by the Allies with increasing annoyance. So precarious did the situation become that on April 5th, 1940, the Germans dispatched troopships disguised as peaceful merchantmen to Norway as a preliminary to invasion. On April 8th the Allies announced that they had mined certain Norwegian territorial waters to prevent the passage of German contraband, and almost before the Norwegian protest had reached London the Germans had invaded Norway.

2. Then the Germans Came

The Germans struck with a speed and efficiency which surprised and dismayed the whole world; their combination of airborne and naval landings gave a foretaste of the real capacity of the Wehrmacht. Within 12 hours they had occupied the capital. Handicapped by years of unpreparedness and "it can't happen here," the Norwegians gave ground into the interior and continued to mobilise, while ill-equipped detachments of Norwegian soldiers armed with rifles and machine-guns fought brave and sometimes successful engagements against German panzers, light artillery and Stukas. Most important of all, the King and Government had escaped from the capital and were making their way north, refusing German demands for surrender. Parliament met first at Hamar, then at Elverum, where a decision of the greatest importance was taken; the Government was given full powers to act for the nation even if it should be compelled to leave the country. But there seemed to be a reasonable hope of holding the Germans—25,000 Norwegians had been mobilised into mountain formations, and Allied troops landed in Norway on April 15th.

3. Allied Aid versus German Reinforcements

Unfortunately, the Allies possessed no air cover and the German inflow of reinforcements proved too heavy; slowly the scales tipped against the Allies; Southern Norway had to be given up; and finally, when things seemed to have stabilised in the North, events in Western Europe forced the Allies to withdraw completely. Sadly the King and Government embarked for England, consoled only by the knowledge that their resourcefulness had saved Norway's constitutional position and gold supplies and had brought the greater part of the Norwegian navy into Allied hands. On June 9th Northern Norway capitulated, and hostilities on Norwegian soil finished. Even so, Norway's resistance of two months lasted longer than that of any other nation which was to be overrun by the Germans: the Germans lost between sixty and seventy thousand men in the course of the campaign, and the German Navy lost so heavily that it emerged little stronger than the Swedish Navy.

4. What was the Nazi Idea?

The Germans' policy for holding Norway, it has now become clear, was to use a Norwegian puppet régime for administering and exploiting the country and to support it by third-rate administrative and technical personnel from Germany. The German aims in Norway appear to have been threefold; in the first place to exploit the country's strategic and military possibilities as a northern flank for their U-boat war and to prevent a flank attack by the Allies, in the second place to secure Norway's economic resources, and in the third place to nazify the population and to incorporate it politically and administratively within "New Europe." The latter aim was to be achieved through Quisling and his supporters.

5. Were There Many Traitors?

The part played by treachery in the conquest of Norway has been greatly exaggerated; undoubtedly Quisling was able to increase the difficulties of Norwegian mobilisation slightly by his fifth column, and one of his lieutenants handed over Narvik to the Germans without resistance, but these were the only two palpable results of the German plans for fifth-columnism. Any benefits to the Germans were completely outweighed by the trouble which they laid up for themselves through choosing as their puppet a shady political adventurer, Vidkun Quisling, whom the Norwegian people would not tolerate as their leader under any circumstances.

III. The Quisling Fiasco

1. Norwegians Are Legal-minded

The first difficulty which the Germans ran into in their efforts to install a puppet régime was the obstinate legal-mindedness of the Norwegians. They attempted to procure the abdication or dismissal of the King and the resignation of Norway's legitimate

Government, but they were unable to find any responsible body of Norwegians who would assist them. The Supreme Court ruled their proposals unconstitutional, and the Administrative Council of loyal Norwegians who ran the country in the absence of the King and Government rejected them; while the King himself, on being approached by the Presidential Board of the Parliament, refused to resign. In September, 1940, the German Reichskommissar Terboven—the highest German authority in Norway—lost patience and cut the Gordian knot by dismissing the Administrative Council, installing Quisling's NS (National Coalition) Party as the only "legitimate" political party in the land, and appointing 13 "Commissary Councillors"—mostly Quislingites— to administer the country under German control.

2. Quisling is a Disappointed Man

From Quisling's point of view the position was hardly satisfactory. True, he could count on valuable support from the Germans. His Party was small, but he could install members in leading positions and thus gain nominal control of all organised life; while the whole Norwegian press and radio was at his disposal for propaganda. His political aims were to promote an "independent" Norway within "New Europe," and to mobilise it alongside Germany in the latter's ideological crusade (Quisling's lunacy was eminently sincere). To do so, he argued, he must obtain a position as Head of State, convince the Norwegians of the legitimacy of his position, conclude peace with Germany, and finally convert the Norwegians to the NS doctrine. Quisling therefore contracted a habit of flying portentously to Berlin to ask for more power and coming back with half-promises from the Nazi Chancellery—half-promises to which a string was always attached, in the form of demands for volunteers for the Eastern Front or for a mobilisation of Norwegian manpower in the name of the "crusade against the terror from the East."

3. Resistance Began At Once

Norwegian Home Front resistance had, however, begun in September, 1940, when Terboven had installed NS as the only "legal" party in the land. This act had shocked the Norwegian people out of the stunned coma into which the invasion and the collapse of the Allied forces in the West had plunged them. Their worst fears confirmed, leading Norwegians in every walk of life began to draw closer together and to exchange views as to the best methods of resisting German penetration. It was clear that in an economically exposed country like Norway, which had lost 50 per cent. of her imports (and those mainly food) through the invasion, guerrilla warfare was an impracticable means of resisting the Germans during an occupation which might last for several years: by the time liberation came, there might well be no Norwegian nation to liberate. The directive which the leaders of Norwegian opinion agreed on, therefore, was to resist the Germans by every form of passive resistance, go-slow, non-collaboration and minor sabotage, and in particular to resist all encroachments on Norwegian legal rights and cultural values.

4. The Church Took a Strong Stand

The Church soon entered the fray to assist the Supreme Court and the jurists. Following a persistent NS campaign of interference with and petty persecution of the clergy, Bishop Berggrav of Oslo—at this time the most powerful figure in the whole of Norway—and his fellow-Bishops declared that they could not continue to hold temporal office under a State that oppressed the Church and that they would resign their temporal duties while retaining their spiritual mandate. The NS promptly announced that Berggrav was dismissed from office and filled the vacant bishoprics with NS clergy. The result was that the Norwegian clergy resigned *en masse* from their temporal offices, and the Norwegian Church "went underground." It still leads spiritual resistance in Norway, headed by a clandestine Temporary Church Council (most of the Bishops, including Berggrav, are under arrest); a small handful of NS clergy preach in empty churches; while the influence of the Church itself on the people is stronger in Norway today than it ever was before.

5. Terror Against Teachers

Another classic example of Home Front resistance was the Schools' struggle. At the end of 1940 the teachers were asked by the Quislingites to adhere to a declaration of loyalty to NS along political lines; 90 per cent. refused. The NS authorities were less delicate about taking action against the teachers than against the clergy, and widespread arrests of teachers took place, as well as demonstrations of brutality by Quisling's "Hirdmen" and the Gestapo. After Quisling's elevation to the Minister-Presidency in February, 1942, new laws were introduced to give the NS control of Norwegian youth. The defence of Norwegian youth against na-zification became a nation-wide issue for teachers, parents, Church and children alike, and in the spring of 1942—the epic period of Norwegian Home Front resistance— they were prepared to make almost any sacrifice to sabotage the NS plans. Over 95 per cent. of Norwegian teachers sent letters to the authorities refusing to remain members of the new-ordered Teachers Association, while over 200,000 parents of families sent letters of protest against the nazification campaign to the "Minister" of Church and Education.

To break this demonstration the Germans emerged from be-hind the NS straw men and employed terror methods. Eleven hundred teachers were arrested, 500 of whom were sent north to work on fortifications in the Arctic; their transport in the tiny steamer *Skjerstad* under shocking conditions is one of the more gruesome stories—though small in scale—of occupied countries in western Europe. The teachers' front held, however, and after some months the teachers were sent home. An uneasy lull still persists, broken by occasional attempts of NS to push through measures which are fiercely resisted by the Home Front.

6. Terror Against Trade Unions

On September 8th, 1941, a strike broke out in Oslo as a protest against the decree forbidding workers to buy milk at their place of work. The Gestapo arrested about 1,000 people, including most of the Trade Union leaders. Two of them, Viggo Hansteen and Rolf Wickstrom, were shot.

7. The Press Went Underground

The clandestine press played a vital part in mobilising Norwegian resistance and transmitting directions to the Norwegian population. In no occupied country have the Germans been more thorough in enforcing the blackout of free news than in Norway. Radio sets were confiscated, and the press and radio controlled. Free speech was forbidden. Without the illegal press, basing its news on the Norwegian broadcasts from the BBC, Norwegian morale could hardly have survived throughout the occupation. Even today, hundreds of different clandestine newspapers are being produced in Norway, and as soon as one paper or ring is broken up another takes its place.

8. The Price Norway Has Paid

Such has been the character of Norwegian Home Front resistance. It has been based on the assumption of an Allied victory, without which the Norwegian case is hopeless; it has in fact been a delaying action fought against nazification. It has only incidentally and in part sabotaged the Germans' twin aims of military and economic exploitation. But it has completely destroyed the German illusion that the Nazi ideology can be implanted in the Norwegian nation. The price paid has not been heavy in comparison with that of (for instance) Greece: but, for a small nation, it has been heavy enough. Some 40,000 Norwegian men and women have been imprisoned, many without trial or examination, and at the moment there are about 12,000 Norwegians in prison or concentration camps. Nearly 4,000 leading personalities have been deported to prison in Germany. Two hundred have been executed and a similar number tortured to death or driven to suicide in prison.

9. Norway's War Effort and Future Outlook

In Norway today peoples' minds turn mainly on liberation and the efforts of their forces abroad. They are gradually beginning to see in broad perspective the enormous part which the Norwegian merchant marine, totalling some 4,000,000 gross tons, manned by 25,000 Norwegian seamen and run by their own legitimate Government, has played in the Allied war effort. Without Norwegian tankers it is difficult to see how Britain could have survived in the Battle of Britain. The Norwegian people have a high—sometimes a too high— estimate of the size of Norway's military forces abroad; her Air Force with its own training schools in Canada, her Army in Britain, and her Navy. They are serenely confident about the achievements of "Free Norway." But, above all, they know what they will want when their country is liberated, and they have a shrewd idea of how to get it. They want a reconstructed Norway, based essentially on her pre-war structure but incorporating additional progressive improvements such as increased collaboration between the various political and social groups, social security, etc. And—so far as the outsider can observe—they are determined to create a national defence and a system of international friendships which will protect them for all the foreseeable future from another German attack. This, it seems likely, will be the greatest thing that Germany has lost from her attack on Norway.

IV. Denmark, a True Democracy

1. Denmark Was Once An Empire

There are places in England where mothers still frighten their children with the Danes. Mothers must have long memories for it is just about 1,000 years since the Danes successfully invaded England. There was a time when Denmark was an Empire and when the name of the Vikings struck terror into the hearts of inhabitants on the western seaboard of Europe. Already then it was demonstrated that aggression does not pay, for after a short spell the Danish rule over England collapsed. Still, the Danish period has left its important traces in the English race, in place names and the language. Englishmen who look at the signposts in certain parts of Denmark often wonder whether they are in Denmark or somewhere on the east coast of England. And as for the language, fishermen from the West Coast of Jutland maintain that they can understand colleagues from certain parts of North England. But then these skippers are men of few words.

Through the ages the history of Denmark has been one of many ups and downs. At one time Danes ruled the whole of Scandinavia; on one occasion only the capital, Copenhagen, was in Danish hands while the rest of the country was overrun. Copenhagen, incidentally, is one of the few European capitals which had never been taken by an enemy until the Germans walked in in 1940.

2. Germany Has Always Been the Enemy

Through the centuries Danes have had to fight their powerful neighbours to the south, the Germans. In recent times Denmark was the first victim of Bismarck's imperialism—in 1864 he seized the frontier Duchy of Slesvig-Holstein, of which the northern part was almost exclusively Danish. The Danes in North Slesvig suffered brutal oppression until they were enabled to return to Denmark in 1920 after a plebiscite under the Versailles treaty. The frontier which was then drawn, in accordance with a free vote, is by most Danes regarded as a just frontier, and there is no Danish desire for territorial expansion at Germany's expense. A small state like Denmark can only hope to exist when it is a homogeneous national unit. Furthermore, Denmark is anxious not to furnish the Germans with an excuse for a future attack, for they believe that the character of the Germans is the same, whether they are headed by a Bismarck, a Kaiser or a Führer. Modern Denmark only counts one potential enemy— Germany.

3. The Story Behind Danish Bacon and Eggs

In peace-time hundreds of people visited Denmark to study the Folk High Schools and the Co-operative system, two things which have been of great importance to the development of the country. Since the first Folk High School was founded 100 years ago, this system of adult education in citizenship has had a profound influence in making the Danish farmers an enlightened community ready to go ahead along new and untested roads. Without the High Schools it is doubtful whether the Co-operative movement would have succeeded. The co-operative idea was borrowed from Britain, but it was developed far beyond anything that has been attempted in this country. Butter and bacon are produced by modern factories run by the farmers themselves on a co-operative basis. Eggs are collected and marketed, and the farmer gets everything from ordinary consumers' goods to artificial manure through his own co-operative organisations. There is one point about this system: every man has the same influence on the affairs of the co-operative society, whether he owns 300 acres or 10. Most Danish farmers, in fact, own their farms, and if the young farmer lacks capital to start for himself the State is there to help him. Without the co-operative system and owner-farming, Danish agriculture would not have reached its present high level.

4. Danish Experiments in Democracy

The co-operative system proved a good training for those who were anxious to play their part in public life. Denmark's smallness has in a way also proved a great asset, for Danes could afford to make social experiments and write them off if they failed without endangering the stability of the State. As a rule they succeeded, particularly the social experiments. In 1932 Denmark carried out her own "Beveridge Plan," and she still holds a place, side by side with Sweden and pre-war Norway, as one of the leading nations in the fields of social security. Social legislation linked with easy access to good education has brought Denmark as near as possible to the "equality in opportunity" which many regard as the definition of democracy.

V. Hitler's Model Protectorate

1. The "New Order" in Denmark

When Hitler invaded Denmark on April 9th, 1940, he met a short, but sharp, resistance. There was no chance of prolonged fighting—the Danish Army was negligible and there was no hope of assistance from outside. The land frontier with Germany and the lack of any natural obstacles made a clear run for Hitler's Panzers, which reached the northern tip of Denmark 200 miles away on the first day of the invasion. The capital is half-an-hour's flying distance from the German airfields on the Baltic, and the German Minister in Copenhagen threatened to obliterate the city unless the Danes gave in. The King and Government ordered the fighting to be stopped—the Germans were masters of the country. The Nazis gave a number of promises: they would respect the Government's rights to settle all internal matters, and they would withdraw after the war. The German soldiers were ordered to behave as human beings, and they did so for a couple of years. The small Danish Nazi Party (40,000) under Frits Clausen were kept in the background.

Why this difference from Norway, where the Germans did all in their power to nazify the country? The most probable explanation is that the Germans wanted to keep Denmark as a show piece to demonstrate to the European nations that Nazi Germany was much better than her reputation. Hitler would use Denmark as a "Model Protectorate" to convince other nations that the war was not really worth fighting, for the Nazis were quite reasonable after all. If the Danes would accept economic collaboration and a certain amount of German political control (in other words, renounce their independence) they were promised a peaceful existence within the German "Lebensraum." The Danish Government and people immediately saw what this meant and refused to enter into any arrangement which would compromise Denmark's future as a free nation. Strangely enough, the Danes were most adamant when things looked blackest for the Allies.

2. Passive Resistance as a Fine Art

In Denmark was assembled more food than the Germans had seen on one spot for years. They laid their hands on it and sent it to Germany. The occupation had created unemployment—the Germans offered to employ the surplus of Danish labour in their war industry. Everything that Denmark could produce would find a ready market in Germany, and the Danish National Bank was forced to pay for it. It was all done in a rather subtle way. When the Germans wanted Danish workers they indicated that they would be unable to deliver coal to Denmark unless Denmark supplied labour. The stopping of coal supplies to Denmark would paralyse all civilised life and cause untold misery, so Danish workers went to Germany. Naturally, they gave the Germans as much trouble as they could without being sent to concentration camps.

Inside Denmark itself passive resistance was developed to a fine art and it was practised by all, from the highest officials to the worker on the German fortifications. It proved an unspectacular, but effective, way of hampering the Germans.

3. Saboteurs Set to Work

The more adventurous Danes were dissatisfied with passive resistance as the main weapon against the intruder, and gradually sabotage was introduced. At first it was amateurish attempts against factories working for the Germans or small-scale attacks on German army installations, but soon sabotage grew so much that the Germans could no longer afford to disregard it.

One effect of sabotage was greatly reduced German exploitation of Danish industry. Industrialists now think twice before they accept a German order, for they know that their plant is likely to be blown up. In November, 1943, there were more than 300 major sabotage cases in Denmark. Some 20 saboteurs have been executed by the Germans, and more have been killed in fighting with German police and sabotage guards, but the struggle goes on.

4. The Germans Struck Back

In August, 1943, the Germans decided to end resistance by the old German means—force. They presented the National Government with a series of demands which the Government refused. On August 29th the Germans struck. Remnants of the Danish army which the Germans had allowed were overpowered in their barracks—the German C.-in-C., General Hanneken, was afraid that the Danish soldiers might attack the Germans in the rear in case of an invasion. The small Danish Navy was to have been seized by the Nazis, but the Navy was ready. Ships which could not make their escape to Sweden scuttled themselves—one after another blew up in the naval docks while the Germans looked on in rage on the quay unable to intervene.

Since then there has been no Government in Denmark, and King Christian is virtually a prisoner in German hands. Resistance continues on an increasing scale, and the last German hope of anything like a working arrangement with the Danes was quashed when the Germans tried to round up the Danish Jews on October 1st, 1943. It is believed that Hitler himself gave the order to arrest and deport to Germany all Jews in Denmark. The result was one of the most spectacular demonstrations of national unity. Every single Dane felt it his duty to come to the assistance of the Jews, and within a week some 6,000 of them were ferried across the sound to Sweden in rowing boats and fishing boats. Only some

600 Jews—most of them too old to escape—were caught by the Germans, and they are now in the Jewish concentration camp of Theresienstadt, in Bohemia.

The 6,000 Jews have since been followed by 8,000 other Danes who fled to safety when the Gestapo were on their track. But as many as possible of the active resistance movement stay behind—there is still a job to do in Denmark.

VI. The Nazi Failure in Denmark

1. Danish Quislings are Few

In spite of the different methods applied by the Germans results were in the end the same as in Norway. The Danish Nazi party was never allowed to play a part in the German scheme, partly because the example from Norway was far from encouraging, partly because a Quisling Government would ruin the myth of a peaceful country. In 1943 the leader of the Danish Nazi party, Dr. Frits Clausen, was forced to volunteer for the Eastern Front because he was unable to account for 100,000 kroner, which the Germans had put at his disposal. He never reached the Eastern Front, for the Germans put him in prison in Berlin for using violence against a nurse. The quality of the ordinary Danish Nazi was just as high as that of his leader.

2. Armed Traitors with Criminal Records

In all occupied countries the Germans have tried to recruit volunteers for fighting against the Russians. In Denmark a few hundred volunteers came forward, and then the recruiting fizzled out. The latest German creation in Denmark is the Schalburg Korps, which clearly is founded with the intention of keeping Danish civilians in order in case of an Allied invasion. These traitors, about 2,000 of them, are the worst possible type of men—half of them have a criminal record. They are responsible for numerous murders of Danish patriots, among them the most outstanding playwright in Scandinavia of our time, Kaj Munk. The Shalburg men will fare badly when the account comes to be settled.

3. The Underground Movement Has Grown

During the first 2 to 3 years of the Occupation the underground movement had a chance to organise itself without serious interference from the Germans. This steady growth has given to Denmark one of the best organised resistance movements in occupied Europe. It keeps the public informed through some 30 illegal papers which appear in spite of all German attempts to track them down. The biggest of these papers have a circulation of 100,000—almost as much as the biggest Copenhagen daily paper. The illegal papers give the news which is withheld from the German-controlled press, they publish black lists of collaborators and generally speaking serve as a great encouragement for the underground movement. Separate groups organise the sabotage under expert guidance.

4. A Council of Freedom Organises Resistance

In September 1943, the resistance groups formed "Denmark's Council of Freedom" which is now the central organisation for all anti-German activity. Recently the Council published a plan for the settlement with traitors and collaborators after the war. This document is significant, because it demonstrates that the fighters in the underground front line have not lost their faith in the ability of a democratic Denmark to settle the matter without resorting to totalitarian methods. According to this plan even the Danish Nazis have a claim to justice.

5. The Free Danes Fight

Shortly after the invasion a Free Danish Movement sprang up in Britain to organise Danish assistance to the Allied cause. The most important contribution is rendered by 6,000 Danish seamen manning 800,000 tons of Danish shipping. Danish volunteers are serving in all the fighting forces, and two small units of the Navy are now manned by Danish seamen.

Denmark is not formally an Ally, but the Free Danes are participating in many negotiations relating to the post-war world, where it is felt that Denmark, in spite of her small size, may yet come to play a part not as a "Model Protectorate," but as an independent democracy.

Current Affairs

NORTHERN NEIGHBOUR

By MAJOR RICHARD BENNETT, R.A.

VOCATIONAL TRAINING

•

No. B6 M.E. EDITION OCTOBER 19th 1945

Northern Neighbour

Norway After the Liberation by Major Richard Bennett, R.A.

(From ABCA Current Affairs, No. B6, October 19th, 1945)

Tromso.

1. BRITONS IN NORWAY—The Germans Surrender

ON June 7th last King Haakon returned to Norway. It was the fifth anniversary of the day when he and the Norwegian Government left for this country during the German invasion of 1940. On the day the King returned, the civil administration of the country was handed over to the Norwegian Government by Shaef, though certain rights such as jurisdiction over Germans and transport facilities were reserved for the Supreme Allied Commander. The formal liberation of the country had taken place a month earlier on May 7th, when the German C.-in-C. in Norway, General Böhme, issued an Order of the Day to his troops announcing the capitulation and containing the words "Unbeaten, in full possession of our strength, we stand in Norway. No enemy has dared to attack us. Yet we, too, must bow to the dictate of our enemies in the wider interest of the cause of Germany."

There were at that time some 500,000 Germans in Norway, including civilians such as Todt workers. This figure alone gives a measure of the problem that faced the Allied military authorities in Norway. The dismantling of a military machine of this size meant more than a little staff work, and, on a lower level, day after day of usually unrewarding chores and guard duties, for, at the beginning, there were less than 10,000 British and American troops—and there were never more than one and a half divisions—to deal with the half million Germans, the 80,000 Russian prisoners of war, and the smaller, but cumulatively large, groups of Poles, Czechs, Yugoslavs, Rumanians, Italians, and even Frenchmen, who had either been imprisoned or forced into service by the Germans.

Norway was No Holiday Camp

What then have we been doing in Norway? The fact that Norway has had one of the pleasantest summers within living memory, that both the Norwegian authorities, families and individuals went to extraordinary lengths to make the stay of Allied forces both pleasant and interesting—as anyone who has been in or near Oslo, for example, can testify—and that the Germans had very considerable stocks of their own and other people's more agreeable drinks, between them have led to reports suggesting that Norway has been little more than a holiday camp. This impression is both unjust and a pity. It is unjust because it is not true. All play and no work has obviously never been on the routine orders of any unit, even in and around the hospitable and friendly centres of population in Southern Norway, and still less in the gaunt and sparse territories in the North. It is a pity because there was a big job to be done and it has been done well, and we might as well take credit for what we achieve in a Europe that is said to be looking towards us for leadership.

The job was mainly to sort and remove the foreigners, both enemies and prisoners of war, from Norwegian soil as quickly as possible. It was a difficult and confusing administrative problem, though on the Civil Affairs side at least there was less work than had been expected. German demolitions were fewer, except in the far North, and the material destruction less, than anywhere else in Europe. Much of the equipment and many of the stores prepared for Norway could be left behind. Petrol, lubricants and coal were the worst shortages, and when the Allies entered the country most of the trains were using wood for fuel. But the ports were nearly all in good condition, and the supply of electric power was plentiful. Food was short but not desperately so. Agriculture was in a tolerable state except for lack of fertilisers. The difficulties were mild compared with those countries which had been fought over, and the diversion of effort towards satisfying essential civilian needs was less than in most other countries.

Unwinding the Wehrmacht

Dealing with the German armies was a formidable task. With so few Allied soldiers to look after so many Germans, it was not possible to disarm, feed and repatriate the enemy unless they were made to do most of the work themselves. This the Germans have done, and with great efficiency. They are not strictly prisoners of war but a disarmed army. They have been in their own formations and under their own discipline but subject to the orders and supervision of the Allies. They have lived on their own reserve stocks of food, swept mines, repaired roads, bridges and quays with their own equipment and assembled, packed and crated their own ammunition. To the unprepared visitor the sight of Germans walking free through the streets of Norwegian towns, unloading ships or working on repairs under their own N.C.Os., or driving British officers in German staff cars was unexpected, and, it must be admitted, naturally unpleasing to those Norwegians, who, for their own reasons, would like to see every German dangling at the end of a rope.

But this was a practical policy and not one to appease a defeated enemy. War criminals and S.S. men have been segregated and put behind well-guarded barbed wire. Generals and senior staff officers, who have fulfilled all the duties required of them by the Allied command, go the same way. Their journey home is not considered strictly necessary for the time being.

The rest must go through a "screening" camp, or "sausage machine," as it is called, before they are repatriated. The Germans are put through in batches of a hundred, and are disposed of at the rate of 1,000—1,500 a day. First they are medically inspected and deloused. Next their kits are searched, and everything above a minimum scale removed from them, including anything acquired by any means in Norway. Next their papers are checked against a constantly increasing card index of "wanted" men. Next they are interrogated to establish whether they are really the people they represent themselves to be. They are not always; generals masquerading as corporals, and Gestapo men and war criminals with faked identities, are weeded out. Those who pass through the filter are herded into closely guarded camps until they are packed, not as units, but as uncomfortable and uneasy individuals into crowded German ships. Such is the inglorious departure of the Wehrmacht from the Northern bastion of their Fortress Europe.

War Criminals and Their Victims

It was better that way. Driving the Germans out of Norway by force of arms would have been an expensive and difficult operation, and both we and the Norwegians may have cause to be glad that it was not necessary. The country was well enough provided and stocked to be the last desperate Nazi rallying point that many people thought it might be before the capitulation. It had been fortified strongly against attack both from the East and the West and at appalling cost in human life to the slave labourers, mostly

In holes in the ground such as these, Russian prisoners of war, employed as slave labour to build Nazi fortifications, starved and froze to death. This camp, one of many, was well inside the Arctic Circle where temperatures fall 40° below zero in the three months of winter darkness.

Russian, who were set to this work. The policy of Belsen and Buchenwald extended as far as the Arctic circle, where Russian prisoners of war, too weak and ill to work, were tortured, murdered, or left to freeze and starve to death in camps in the farthest North. Seeking out and caging the authors of these inhumanities has been another of our responsibilities.

The End of a Difficult Job

But disposing of the Germans was not the only problem that faced General Thorne, the Allied Commander. There were also the victims to deal with. There were still 80,000 Russian prisoners of war alive in Norway after the capitulation. They had to be cared for, clothed and repatriated. Many of them, as may be imagined, were in a deplorable condition. But there were also groups of men varying in size from some thousands to a few hundred from more than half a dozen countries. They were the pitiable backwash of the Nazi career across Europe. Some were prisoners of war, others, members of the Todt organization, or forcibly impressed or voluntary members of the Wehrmacht. All of them presented separate problems, not so large as that of the Germans, but frequently more complicated both administratively and politically.

All this has been hard work for the comparative handful of men engaged on it, particularly those in the North. From the far North to well South of Trondheim there were only two converted A.A. Brigades, the 303 and 304 Infantry Brigades. They had the largest numbers of Germans, prisoners of war and displaced persons to deal with, and the maximum amount of initial chaos to reduce to order. There were few towns in their area, and of them only Trondheim offered any real possibility of social life. The British troops there bore their hard work and frequently severe, beautiful but socially forbidding surroundings cheerfully, except perhaps when they read reports in week-old newspapers of the wonderful time they were having. But the military job in Norway is now drawing towards its close. Soon all that will remain to be done will be to remove ourselves, the last foreigners from Norwegian soil, and to leave the Norwegians at long last in sole and undisputed possession of their country.

2. NORWEGIANS AT HOME—German Occupation was Thorough

Now that the Norwegians are masters once more in their own house, it is perhaps worth considering the domestic problems that beset this small friendly neighbour who has contributed so much to the Allied cause both in men and ships. First of all there are the problems created by five years of German occupation. Half a million Germans may seem a large but not an excessive number until you remember the population of Norway is less than three millions. If we had been invaded and occupied on the same scale the number of Germans in the United Kingdom would have been between seven and eight millions. The saturation of Norway by Germans was, thus, intensive, more intensive, perhaps, than in any other occupied territory. Even when the number of Germans in Norway was half and even less of the final figure the proportion of adult Germans to adult able-bodied Norwegians capable of active resistance was always extraordinarily high. In some areas, even, the Norwegians were living with the Germans rather than the Germans with the Norwegians. They will tell you in Narvik, for example, that there were more German servicemen quartered in and around the town than there were Norwegian men, women and children put together. This consideration, and the geography and climate of the country, prevented widespread guerrilla activity against the Germans, and largely dictated the character of Norwegian resistance.

The Resistance Helped the Transition to Peace

Nevertheless there was an effective and nation-wide resistance movement. It ran an intelligence service which reported to London military and naval dispositions and the movements of troops, ships and submarines. The military wing of the resistance sent men out of the country to join the Norwegian forces overseas and trained others at home in the use of arms in preparation for a day that, fortunately for Norway, never came. We should also remember that we have Norwegians to thank for the destruction of the heavy-water plant near Rjukan in Telemark. This coup prevented the possibility of Germany producing an atomic bomb. The civil wing ran illegal newspapers, kept tabs on the Quislings, informed the home front leadership, as the controlling committee was called, of conditions throughout the country. It also organized collections and food supplies for the victims of the Gestapo. For all this work had to be done with the Germans on top of them, and many brave men and women either lost their lives or were sent to concentration camps. In July, 1944, there were 6,000 Norwegians in concentration camps in Germany and another 6,000 in Norway. It is known that these figures grew considerably later. Nevertheless the resistance was never broken up, and the leadership had a sufficiently centralized organization to make the transition from occupation to liberation smoother than in many other parts of Europe, and there has so far been little sign in Norway of the new cleavage, familiar elsewhere, between the resistance and the returning government.

The Economic and Social Hangover

Still there are other problems. Economically the Germans plundered the country. They did not destroy it, but milked it dry. Norway had been a well-stocked country before the war. The cost of the occupation fell heavily upon the Norwegians. Two-thirds of their national income was eaten up in providing for these most unwelcome guests. It was estimated that up to the end of August, 1944, the occupation had cost the Norwegians £47 a head. Equivalent figures for other occupied countries were Denmark: £25 5s., Holland £7 6s., France and Belgium £5. Food was short. Shops were empty. In the far North there were even people who had to go through the long Arctic winter without light.

At the same time the Germans were the direct employers of about 150,000 Norwegians. Workers must work to live whoever is the master. They paid them good wages. They paid farmers good prices for their produce. It was not difficult or expensive for they merely increased the Norwegian note circulation to do so. The combination of plunder and manipulation of the note issue has left Norway a country in which there is on the whole plenty of money and almost nothing to buy. One natural but serious economic consequence has been a reluctance to go to work since the liberation. This has considerably slowed down the tempo of reconstruction.

Socially, five years of German occupation has created antagonisms within Norwegian society, as everywhere else. The Quislings are an obvious example. They present a clear cut problem. Between 15 and 16 thousand suspects have been arrested in all, most of them for quite minor acts of collaboration. The trials are going on now. The Norwegian mothers of the 7–8,000 German fathered children are a separate and smaller problem, but obviously they are resented.

People who were strong-minded enough not to, or lucky enough not to have been forced to work for the Germans tend to regard those who did as collaborators. There are even minor but occasional differences between those who stayed behind and those who left the country. Education has suffered in these five years, if only because teachers tended to attract the attention of the Gestapo, and school buildings the requisitioning appetite of the Wehrmacht. Many of the young people who grew up to working age during the occupation went to work for the Germans. In many places there was no one else to work for. They have been used to earning what seemed relatively good money, but have not mastered the simple truth that money is only worth what it will buy. Many older Norwegians feel that a section of their youth has been temporarily corrupted by the Germans, and estranged from the old way of life.

Norway's Recovery Depends on Others as Well

There are still other problems. Norway before the war was a small country with a high standard of living, which depended more than any country in the world, with the possible exception of New Zealand, on imports. She imported more than she exported, but was able to cover the difference with the money earned by her mercantile marine, which was the fourth largest in the world. To-day the balance of imports over exports is disproportionately heavy. In June, for example, Norway imported goods from Sweden to the value of 120 million kroner and only exported 12 millions. A man-power crisis is at present reducing her main industry, wood pulp and paper, to 40 per cent. of its capacity. The iron ore mines have been largely destroyed by the war and are not likely to be in full production until next summer. Germany, which used to be Norway's second best customer, is not in a position to buy anything, and fresh markets have to be found for the goods, particularly salted herrings, which used to go to Germany.

Norway's problem, like every other country's, depends therefore not only on internal stability but on the general post-war settlement. Half her ships, which have been serving with the Allies, have been sunk, and the insurance money is locked up in this country. So Norway's quick recovery depends also on ours, both in this special sense, and in the sense that we were her best customer before the war.

Thus many of Norway's immediate problems are not very different from ours. The Norwegians are in for a hard and difficult, but not a desperate, winter. Consumption goods are very short. Clothes and shoes made from paper are on sale in many shops. They have to build up their stocks and their export industries as soon as possible. In one respect they are lucky. They have less material destruction to repair than any other European belligerent, except in Finnmark in the far North. There the Germans, retreating from Finland before the Russians in the last winter of the war, destroyed every farmstead, slaughtered the cattle, blew all the bridges and mined and cratered the roads. It is the poorest part of Norway, and is inhabited by a mixed population of Norwegians, Finns, and Lapps. So Finnmark, at least, presents a melancholy and difficult problem of physical reconstruction.

The First Steps Towards a Secure Future

Meanwhile the Norwegians do not appear to be downhearted, and the Government has intervened to prevent any prolongation of the holiday spirit that has prevailed since the liberation. The former bank-notes issued by the Bank of Norway and printed in Norway during the occupation ceased to be legal tender on September 8th. They had to be handed in to the authorities before September 22nd, or, abroad, before October 6th. Each ration card holder will be allowed new notes to a value of 100 kroner (£5). Old notes will be exchanged for new ones up to a value of 5,000 kroner. Sums exceeding this amount will be entered on a special account which can be realized later. Those who hand in too many notes may have some difficult explanations to make, and everyone will once more have to work for a living. The whole operation, in the words of the Minister of Finance, is an experiment to help create stability in economic life and enable a start to be made in the reconstruction of the country.

That has been the first step forward, and on October 8th Norwegians go to the polls to choose the Government that will guide them on the next stage into the future.

www.ingramcontent.com/pod-product-compliance
Lightning Source LLC
Chambersburg PA
CBHW060633030426
42337CB00018B/3346